# Longer Calendars
## for Wider Outlooks
## 18-MONTH PLANNER

Activinotes

## Activinotes

DAILY JOURNALS, PLANNERS, NOTEBOOKS AND OTHER BLANK BOOKS

| Monday | | Friday | |
|---|---|---|---|

things to do

_____
_____
_____
_____

| Tuesday | | Saturday | |
|---|---|---|---|

things to buy

_____
_____
_____
_____
_____

| Wednesday | | Sunday | |
|---|---|---|---|

| Thursday | |
|---|---|

Notes

_____
_____
_____
_____
_____

# Weekly Planner

| Monday | | Friday | |

Monday

Friday

Tuesday

Saturday

Wednesday

Sunday

Thursday

things to do

_____
_____
_____
_____
_____
_____

things to buy

_____
_____
_____
_____
_____
_____

Notes

_____
_____
_____
_____
_____
_____

# Weekly Planner

things to do

_____
_____
_____
_____
_____
_____
_____

things to buy

_____
_____
_____
_____
_____
_____

Notes

_____
_____
_____
_____
_____
_____
_____

Monday

Tuesday

Wednesday

Thursday

Friday

Saturday

Sunday

# Weekly Planner

| Monday | | Friday | |

| Tuesday | | Saturday | |

| Wednesday | | Sunday | |

| Thursday | |

things to do

_____

_____

_____

_____

_____

_____

_____

things to buy

_____

_____

_____

_____

_____

_____

_____

Notes

_____

_____

_____

_____

_____

_____

# Weekly Planner

things to do

_____
_____
_____
_____
_____
_____
_____

things to buy

_____
_____
_____
_____
_____
_____

Notes

_____
_____
_____
_____
_____
_____

| Monday | | Thursday | |
|---|---|---|---|
| Tuesday | | Friday | |
| Wednesday | | Saturday | |
| | | Sunday | |

# Weekly Planner

Grocery List

_____
_____
_____
_____
_____

Contact Number

_____
_____
_____
_____
_____

Reminders

_____
_____
_____
_____
_____
_____
_____
_____
_____
_____
_____
_____
_____
_____

Notes

Weekly Planner

Monday

Friday

Tuesday

Saturday

Wednesday

Sunday

Thursday

things to do

_____
_____
_____
_____
_____
_____
_____

things to buy

_____
_____
_____
_____
_____
_____
_____

Notes

_____
_____
_____
_____
_____
_____

# Weekly Planner

| Monday | | Friday | |
|---|---|---|---|
| Tuesday | | Saturday | |
| Wednesday | | Sunday | |
| Thursday | | | |

_____
_____
_____
_____
_____
_____
_____

things to buy

_____
_____
_____
_____
_____
_____

## Notes

_____
_____
_____
_____
_____

# Weekly Planner

things to do

_____

_____

_____

_____

_____

_____

things to buy

_____

_____

_____

_____

_____

Notes

_____

_____

_____

_____

_____

_____

_____

| Monday | | Thursday | |
|---|---|---|---|
| Tuesday | | Friday | |
| Wednesday | | Saturday | |
| | | Sunday | |

# Weekly Planner

| | | |
|---|---|---|
| **Monday** | | **Friday** |
| **Tuesday** | | **Saturday** |
| **Wednesday** | | **Sunday** |
| **Thursday** | | |

**things to do**

_____
_____
_____
_____
_____
_____
_____

**things to buy**

_____
_____
_____
_____
_____
_____

**Notes**

_____
_____
_____
_____
_____
_____

# Weekly Planner

things to do

_____
_____
_____
_____
_____
_____
_____

things to buy

_____
_____
_____
_____
_____
_____

Notes

_____
_____
_____
_____
_____
_____

| Monday | | Thursday | |
| Tuesday | | Friday | |
| Wednesday | | Saturday | |
| | | Sunday | |

# Weekly Planner

## Grocery List

_____

_____

_____

_____

_____

_____

_____

_____

_____

_____

_____

_____

_____

_____

_____

_____

_____

_____

## Reminders

_____

_____

_____

_____

_____

_____

_____

_____

_____

_____

_____

_____

## Contact Number

_____

_____

_____

_____

_____

_____

_____

_____

_____

_____

_____

_____

_____

## Notes

| | |
|---|---|
| Monday | Friday |
| Tuesday | Saturday |
| Wednesday | Sunday |
| Thursday | |

things to do

_____
_____
_____
_____
_____
_____

things to buy

_____
_____
_____
_____
_____
_____

Notes

_____
_____
_____
_____
_____
_____

# Weekly Planner

**Monday**

**Tuesday**

**Wednesday**

**Thursday**

**Friday**

**Saturday**

**Sunday**

things to do

_____
_____
_____
_____
_____
_____
_____

things to buy

_____
_____
_____
_____
_____
_____
_____

Notes

_____
_____
_____
_____
_____
_____

# Weekly Planner

things to do

_____

_____

_____

_____

_____

_____

_____

things to buy

_____

_____

_____

_____

_____

Notes

_____

_____

_____

_____

_____

_____

| Monday | | Thursday | |
|---|---|---|---|
| Tuesday | | Friday | |
| Wednesday | | Saturday | |
| | | Sunday | |

# Weekly Planner

| | | | |
|---|---|---|---|
| Monday | | Friday | |
| Tuesday | | Saturday | |
| Wednesday | | Sunday | |
| Thursday | | | |

things to do

_____
_____
_____
_____
_____
_____
_____

things to buy

_____
_____
_____
_____
_____
_____
_____

Notes

_____
_____
_____
_____
_____
_____

# Weekly Planner

things to do

_____
_____
_____
_____
_____
_____

things to buy

_____
_____
_____
_____
_____

Notes

_____
_____
_____
_____
_____
_____

| Monday | | Thursday | |
|--------|--|----------|--|
| Tuesday | | Friday | |
| Wednesday | | Saturday | |
| | | Sunday | |

# Weekly Planner

## Grocery List

_____
_____
_____
_____
_____
_____
_____
_____
_____
_____
_____
_____
_____
_____

## Reminders

_____
_____
_____
_____
_____
_____
_____
_____
_____
_____
_____
_____

## Contact Number

_____
_____
_____
_____
_____
_____
_____
_____
_____
_____
_____
_____
_____
_____

## Notes

| Monday | | Friday | |
|---|---|---|---|
| Tuesday | | Saturday | |
| Wednesday | | Sunday | |
| Thursday | | | |

**things to do**

_____
_____
_____
_____
_____
_____
_____

**things to buy**

_____
_____
_____
_____
_____
_____

**Notes**

_____
_____
_____
_____
_____
_____

# Weekly Planner

| Monday | | Friday | |
|---|---|---|---|

**Tuesday** | **Saturday**

**Wednesday** | **Sunday**

**Thursday**

_____
_____
_____
_____
_____
_____

things to buy

_____
_____
_____
_____
_____
_____
_____

Notes
_____
_____
_____
_____
_____
_____

# Weekly Planner

things to do

_____
_____
_____
_____
_____
_____
_____

things to buy

_____
_____
_____
_____
_____
_____

Notes

_____
_____
_____
_____
_____
_____
_____

Monday

Tuesday

Wednesday

Thursday

Friday

Saturday

Sunday

# Weekly Planner

Monday

Tuesday

Wednesday

Thursday

Friday

Saturday

Sunday

things to do

things to buy

Notes

# Weekly Planner

things to do

_____
_____
_____
_____
_____
_____
_____

things to buy

_____
_____
_____
_____
_____
_____

Notes

_____
_____
_____
_____
_____
_____

Monday

Tuesday

Wednesday

Thursday

Friday

Saturday

Sunday

# Weekly Planner

## Grocery List

_____
_____
_____
_____
_____
_____
_____
_____
_____
_____
_____
_____
_____
_____
_____
_____
_____
_____
_____

## Reminders

_____
_____
_____
_____
_____
_____
_____
_____
_____
_____
_____
_____
_____
_____
_____
_____

## Contact Number

_____
_____
_____
_____
_____
_____
_____
_____
_____
_____
_____
_____
_____
_____
_____
_____
_____
_____

## Notes

| Monday | | Friday | |

things to do

_____
_____
_____
_____
_____
_____
_____

| Tuesday | | Saturday | |

things to buy

_____
_____
_____
_____
_____

| Wednesday | | Sunday | |

| Thursday | |

Notes

_____
_____
_____
_____
_____

# Weekly Planner

| | |
|---|---|
| Monday | Friday |
| Tuesday | Saturday |
| Wednesday | Sunday |
| Thursday | |

things to do
_____
_____
_____
_____
_____
_____
_____

things to buy
_____
_____
_____
_____
_____
_____

Notes
_____
_____
_____
_____
_____

# Weekly Planner

things to do

_____
_____
_____
_____
_____
_____
_____

things to buy

_____
_____
_____
_____
_____
_____

Notes

_____
_____
_____
_____
_____
_____

| Monday | | Thursday | |
| Tuesday | | Friday | |
| Wednesday | | Saturday | |
| | | Sunday | |

# Weekly Planner

| | | | |
|---|---|---|---|
| **Monday** | | **Friday** | |
| **Tuesday** | | **Saturday** | |
| **Wednesday** | | **Sunday** | |
| **Thursday** | | | |

**things to do**

_____
_____
_____
_____
_____

**things to buy**

_____
_____
_____
_____
_____

**Notes**

_____
_____
_____
_____
_____
_____

# Weekly Planner

things to do

_____
_____
_____
_____
_____
_____

things to buy

_____
_____
_____
_____
_____

Notes

_____
_____
_____
_____
_____
_____

Monday

Tuesday

Wednesday

Thursday

Friday

Saturday

Sunday

# Weekly Planner

### Grocery List

_____

_____

_____

_____

_____

_____

_____

_____

_____

_____

_____

_____

_____

_____

_____

_____

### Reminders

_____

_____

_____

_____

_____

_____

_____

_____

_____

_____

### Contact Number

_____

_____

_____

_____

_____

_____

_____

_____

_____

_____

_____

_____

_____

_____

_____

_____

### Notes

| | |
|---|---|
| **Monday** | **Friday** |
| **Tuesday** | **Saturday** |
| **Wednesday** | **Sunday** |
| **Thursday** | |

**things to do**

_____
_____
_____
_____
_____
_____
_____

**things to buy**

_____
_____
_____
_____
_____
_____
_____

**Notes**

_____
_____
_____
_____
_____
_____

# Weekly Planner

| | | | |
|---|---|---|---|
| **Monday** | | **Friday** | |
| **Tuesday** | | **Saturday** | |
| **Wednesday** | | **Sunday** | |
| **Thursday** | | | |

things to do

_____
_____
_____
_____
_____
_____

things to buy

_____
_____
_____
_____
_____
_____

Notes

_____
_____
_____
_____
_____
_____

# Weekly Planner

things to do

_____

_____

_____

_____

_____

_____

_____

things to buy

_____

_____

_____

_____

_____

Notes

_____

_____

_____

_____

_____

_____

| Monday | | Thursday | |
|---|---|---|---|
| Tuesday | | Friday | |
| Wednesday | | Saturday | |
| | | Sunday | |

# Weekly Planner

| Monday | | Friday |
| --- | --- | --- |
| **Tuesday** | | **Saturday** |
| **Wednesday** | | **Sunday** |
| **Thursday** | | |

things to do
_____
_____
_____
_____
_____
_____
_____

things to buy
_____
_____
_____
_____
_____
_____
_____

Notes
_____
_____
_____
_____
_____
_____

# Weekly Planner

things to do

_____
_____
_____
_____
_____
_____
_____

things to buy

_____
_____
_____
_____
_____
_____
_____

Notes

_____
_____
_____
_____
_____
_____
_____

Monday

Tuesday

Wednesday

Thursday

Friday

Saturday

Sunday

# Weekly Planner

## Grocery List

_____
_____
_____
_____
_____

## Reminders

_____
_____
_____
_____
_____
_____
_____
_____
_____
_____
_____
_____
_____
_____
_____
_____

## Contact Number

_____
_____
_____
_____

## Notes

| Monday | | Friday | |
|---|---|---|---|
| Tuesday | | Saturday | |
| Wednesday | | Sunday | |
| Thursday | | | |

things to do

_____
_____
_____
_____
_____
_____
_____

things to buy

_____
_____
_____
_____
_____
_____

Notes

_____
_____
_____
_____
_____
_____

# Weekly Planner

| Monday | | Friday | |
|--------|--|--------|--|
| **Monday** | | **Friday** | |
| **Tuesday** | | **Saturday** | |
| **Wednesday** | | **Sunday** | |
| **Thursday** | | | |

_____
_____
_____
_____
_____
_____
_____

**things to buy**

_____
_____
_____
_____
_____
_____

## Notes

_____
_____
_____
_____
_____
_____

# Weekly Planner

things to do

_____
_____
_____
_____
_____
_____

things to buy

_____
_____
_____
_____
_____
_____

Notes

_____
_____
_____
_____
_____
_____
_____

| Monday | | Thursday | |
| Tuesday | | Friday | |
| Wednesday | | Saturday | |
| | | Sunday | |

# Weekly Planner

| Monday | | Friday | |
|---|---|---|---|
| Tuesday | | Saturday | |
| Wednesday | | Sunday | |
| Thursday | | | |

things to do

_____
_____
_____
_____
_____
_____
_____

things to buy

_____
_____
_____
_____
_____
_____
_____

Notes

_____
_____
_____
_____
_____
_____

# Weekly Planner

things to do

_____
_____
_____
_____
_____
_____

things to buy

_____
_____
_____
_____

Notes

_____
_____
_____
_____
_____
_____

| Monday | | Thursday | |
|---|---|---|---|
| Tuesday | | Friday | |
| Wednesday | | Saturday | |
| | | Sunday | |

# Weekly Planner

## Grocery List

_____

_____

_____

_____

_____

_____

_____

_____

_____

_____

_____

_____

_____

_____

_____

_____

## Reminders

_____

_____

_____

_____

_____

_____

_____

_____

_____

_____

_____

_____

_____

_____

## Contact Number

_____

_____

_____

_____

_____

_____

_____

_____

_____

_____

_____

_____

_____

_____

## Notes

| Monday | | Friday |
|---|---|---|
| Tuesday | | Saturday |
| Wednesday | | Sunday |
| Thursday | | |

**things to do**

_____
_____
_____
_____
_____
_____

**things to buy**

_____
_____
_____
_____
_____
_____

**Notes**

_____
_____
_____
_____
_____

# Weekly Planner

| Monday | | Friday | |
|---|---|---|---|
| **Tuesday** | | **Saturday** | |
| **Wednesday** | | **Sunday** | |
| **Thursday** | | | |

things to do
_____
_____
_____
_____
_____
_____
_____

things to buy
_____
_____
_____
_____
_____
_____
_____

Notes
_____
_____
_____
_____
_____
_____

# Weekly Planner

things to do

_____

_____

_____

_____

_____

_____

things to buy

_____

_____

_____

_____

_____

_____

Notes

_____

_____

_____

_____

_____

_____

Monday

Tuesday

Wednesday

Thursday

Friday

Saturday

Sunday

# Weekly Planner

| Monday | | Friday | |
|---|---|---|---|
| Tuesday | | Saturday | |
| Wednesday | | Sunday | |
| Thursday | | | |

things to do

_____
_____
_____
_____
_____
_____
_____
_____

things to buy

_____
_____
_____
_____
_____
_____
_____
_____

Notes

_____
_____
_____
_____
_____
_____

# Weekly Planner

things to do

_____

_____

_____

_____

_____

_____

_____

things to buy

_____

_____

_____

_____

_____

Notes

_____

_____

_____

_____

_____

_____

_____

Monday

Tuesday

Wednesday

Thursday

Friday

Saturday

Sunday

# Weekly Planner

## Grocery List

_____
_____
_____
_____
_____
_____
_____
_____
_____
_____
_____
_____
_____
_____
_____
_____
_____
_____

## Reminders

_____
_____
_____
_____
_____
_____
_____
_____
_____
_____
_____
_____
_____
_____

## Contact Number

_____
_____
_____
_____
_____
_____
_____
_____
_____
_____
_____
_____
_____
_____
_____
_____
_____

## Notes

# 09 September

Weekly Planner

Monday

Friday

Tuesday

Saturday

Wednesday

Sunday

Thursday

things to do

_____

_____

_____

_____

_____

_____

things to buy

_____

_____

_____

_____

_____

_____

Notes

_____

_____

_____

_____

_____

_____

# Weekly Planner

Monday

Tuesday

Wednesday

Thursday

Friday

Saturday

Sunday

things to do

_____

_____

_____

_____

_____

_____

things to buy

_____

_____

_____

_____

_____

_____

Notes

_____

_____

_____

_____

_____

_____

# Weekly Planner

things to do

_____

_____

_____

_____

_____

_____

_____

things to buy

_____

_____

_____

_____

_____

_____

_____

Notes

_____

_____

_____

_____

_____

_____

_____

Monday

Tuesday

Wednesday

Thursday

Friday

Saturday

Sunday

# Weekly Planner

| | | | |
|---|---|---|---|
| **Monday** | | **Friday** | |
| **Tuesday** | | **Saturday** | |
| **Wednesday** | | **Sunday** | |
| **Thursday** | | | |

### things to do

_____

_____

_____

_____

_____

_____

### things to buy

_____

_____

_____

_____

_____

_____

### Notes

_____

_____

_____

_____

_____

_____

# Weekly Planner

things to do

_____

_____

_____

_____

_____

_____

things to buy

_____

_____

_____

_____

_____

Notes

_____

_____

_____

_____

_____

_____

Monday

Tuesday

Wednesday

Thursday

Friday

Saturday

Sunday

# Weekly Planner

Grocery List

_____

_____

_____

_____

_____

_____

_____

_____

_____

_____

_____

_____

_____

_____

_____

_____

Contact Number

_____

_____

_____

_____

_____

_____

_____

_____

_____

_____

_____

Reminders

_____

_____

_____

_____

_____

_____

_____

_____

_____

_____

_____

_____

_____

_____

Notes

# 10 October

Weekly Planner

| | |
|---|---|
| Monday | Friday |
| Tuesday | Saturday |
| Wednesday | Sunday |
| Thursday | |

things to do

_____
_____
_____
_____

_____
_____

things to buy

_____
_____
_____
_____
_____
_____

Notes

_____
_____
_____
_____
_____
_____

# Weekly Planner

| | | | |
|---|---|---|---|
| **Monday** | | **Friday** | |
| **Tuesday** | | **Saturday** | |
| **Wednesday** | | **Sunday** | |
| **Thursday** | | | |

**things to do**

_____
_____
_____
_____
_____
_____
_____

**things to buy**

_____
_____
_____
_____
_____
_____
_____

Notes

_____
_____
_____
_____
_____
_____

# Weekly Planner

things to do

_____
_____
_____
_____
_____
_____
_____

things to buy

_____
_____
_____
_____
_____
_____

Notes

_____
_____
_____
_____
_____
_____

Monday

Tuesday

Wednesday

Thursday

Friday

Saturday

Sunday

# Weekly Planner

| | |
|---|---|
| **Monday** | **Friday** |
| **Tuesday** | **Saturday** |
| **Wednesday** | **Sunday** |
| **Thursday** | |

## things to do

_____

_____

_____

_____

_____

_____

_____

## things to buy

_____

_____

_____

_____

_____

_____

## Notes

_____

_____

_____

_____

_____

_____

# Weekly Planner

things to do

_____

_____

_____

_____

_____

_____

_____

things to buy

_____

_____

_____

_____

_____

Notes

_____

_____

_____

_____

_____

_____

| Monday | | Thursday | |
| Tuesday | | Friday | |
| Wednesday | | Saturday | |
| | | Sunday | |

# Weekly Planner

## Grocery List

_____

_____

_____

_____

_____

## Reminders

_____

_____

_____

_____

_____

_____

_____

_____

_____

_____

_____

_____

_____

_____

## Contact Number

_____

_____

_____

_____

## Notes

# 11 *November*

Monday

Friday

Tuesday

Saturday

Wednesday

Sunday

Thursday

things to do

_____
_____
_____
_____
_____
_____
_____
_____

things to buy

_____
_____
_____
_____
_____
_____
_____

Notes

_____
_____
_____
_____
_____
_____

# Weekly Planner

| | |
|---|---|
| Monday | Friday |
| Tuesday | Saturday |
| Wednesday | Sunday |
| Thursday | |

things to do

_____
_____
_____
_____
_____
_____
_____

things to buy

_____
_____
_____
_____
_____
_____
_____

Notes
_____
_____
_____
_____
_____

# Weekly Planner

things to do

_____
_____
_____
_____
_____
_____
_____

things to buy

_____
_____
_____
_____
_____

Notes

_____
_____
_____
_____
_____
_____

Monday

Tuesday

Wednesday

Thursday

Friday

Saturday

Sunday

# Weekly Planner

**Monday**

**Tuesday**

**Wednesday**

**Thursday**

**Friday**

**Saturday**

**Sunday**

things to do

things to buy

Notes

# Weekly Planner

things to do

_____
_____
_____
_____
_____
_____
_____

things to buy

_____
_____
_____
_____
_____
_____

Notes

_____
_____
_____
_____
_____
_____

Monday

Tuesday

Wednesday

Thursday

Friday

Saturday

Sunday

# Weekly Planner

## Grocery List

_____
_____
_____
_____
_____

## Reminders

_____
_____
_____
_____
_____
_____
_____
_____
_____
_____
_____
_____
_____
_____

## Contact Number

_____
_____
_____
_____
_____
_____

## Notes

| Monday | | Friday | |
|---|---|---|---|
| Tuesday | | Saturday | |
| Wednesday | | Sunday | |
| Thursday | | | |

things to do

_____
_____
_____
_____
_____
_____

things to buy

_____
_____
_____
_____
_____
_____

Notes

_____
_____
_____
_____
_____

# Weekly Planner

| | |
|---|---|
| Monday | Friday |
| Tuesday | Saturday |
| Wednesday | Sunday |
| Thursday | |

_____

_____

_____

_____

_____

_____

things to buy

_____

_____

_____

_____

_____

_____

Notes

_____

_____

_____

_____

_____

_____

# Weekly Planner

things to do

_____

_____

_____

_____

_____

_____

things to buy

_____

_____

_____

_____

Notes

_____

_____

_____

_____

_____

_____

| Monday | | Thursday | |
| Tuesday | | Friday | |
| Wednesday | | Saturday | |
| | | Sunday | |

# Weekly Planner

| Monday | | Friday | |
|---|---|---|---|
| **Tuesday** | | **Saturday** | |
| **Wednesday** | | **Sunday** | |
| **Thursday** | | | |

things to do
_____
_____
_____
_____
_____
_____
_____

things to buy
_____
_____
_____
_____
_____
_____

Notes
_____
_____
_____
_____
_____

# Weekly Planner

things to do

_____
_____
_____
_____
_____
_____

things to buy

_____
_____
_____
_____
_____

Notes

_____
_____
_____
_____
_____
_____

| Monday | | Thursday | |
|---|---|---|---|
| Tuesday | | Friday | |
| Wednesday | | Saturday | |
| | | Sunday | |

# Weekly Planner

## Grocery List

_____
_____
_____
_____
_____
_____
_____
_____
_____
_____
_____
_____
_____
_____
_____
_____

## Reminders

_____
_____
_____
_____
_____
_____
_____
_____
_____
_____
_____
_____

## Contact Number

_____
_____
_____
_____
_____
_____
_____
_____
_____
_____
_____
_____
_____
_____
_____

## Notes

# Weekly Planner

### Grocery List

_____
_____
_____
_____
_____
_____
_____
_____
_____
_____
_____
_____
_____
_____
_____
_____
_____
_____

### Reminders

_____
_____
_____
_____
_____
_____
_____
_____
_____
_____
_____
_____

### Contact Number

_____
_____
_____
_____
_____
_____
_____
_____
_____
_____
_____
_____
_____
_____

### Notes

# Weekly Planner

## Grocery List

_____

_____

_____

_____

_____

_____

_____

_____

_____

_____

_____

_____

_____

_____

_____

_____

_____

## Reminders

_____

_____

_____

_____

_____

_____

_____

_____

_____

_____

_____

_____

## Contact Number

_____

_____

_____

_____

_____

_____

_____

_____

_____

_____

_____

_____

_____

_____

_____

_____

_____

## Notes

# Weekly Planner

## Grocery List

_____
_____
_____
_____
_____
_____
_____
_____
_____
_____
_____
_____
_____
_____
_____
_____
_____
_____

## Reminders

_____
_____
_____
_____
_____
_____
_____
_____
_____
_____
_____
_____
_____

## Contact Number

_____
_____
_____
_____
_____
_____
_____
_____
_____
_____
_____
_____
_____
_____
_____
_____

## Notes

# Weekly Planner

## Grocery List

_____
_____
_____
_____
_____
_____
_____
_____
_____
_____
_____
_____
_____
_____
_____
_____
_____

## Reminders

_____
_____
_____
_____
_____
_____
_____
_____
_____
_____
_____
_____
_____
_____

## Contact Number

_____
_____
_____
_____
_____
_____
_____
_____
_____
_____
_____
_____
_____
_____
_____
_____
_____

## Notes

Longer
Calendars

Plus
Months

# 01 January

Weekly Planner

| Monday | Friday |
| Tuesday | Saturday |
| Wednesday | Sunday |
| Thursday | |

**things to do**

_____
_____
_____
_____
_____
_____
_____

**things to buy**

_____
_____
_____
_____
_____
_____

**Notes**

_____
_____
_____
_____
_____
_____

# Weekly Planner

things to do

_____
_____
_____
_____
_____
_____

things to buy

_____
_____
_____
_____
_____

Notes

_____
_____
_____
_____
_____
_____

Monday

Tuesday

Wednesday

Thursday

Friday

Saturday

Sunday

# Weekly Planner

Monday

Tuesday

Wednesday

Thursday

Friday

Saturday

Sunday

things to do

_____

_____

_____

_____

_____

_____

_____

things to buy

_____

_____

_____

_____

_____

_____

_____

Notes

_____

_____

_____

_____

_____

# Weekly Planner

things to do

_____
_____
_____
_____

_____
_____
_____

things to buy

_____
_____
_____
_____
_____
_____

Notes

_____
_____
_____
_____
_____
_____
_____

Monday

Tuesday

Wednesday

Thursday

Friday

Saturday

Sunday

| | |
|---|---|
| **Monday** | **Friday** |
| **Tuesday** | **Saturday** |
| **Wednesday** | **Sunday** |
| **Thursday** | |

**things to do**

_____
_____
_____
_____
_____
_____
_____

**things to buy**

_____
_____
_____
_____
_____
_____

**Notes**

_____
_____
_____
_____
_____

# Weekly Planner

things to do

_____
_____
_____
_____
_____
_____
_____

things to buy

_____
_____
_____
_____
_____
_____

Notes

_____
_____
_____
_____
_____
_____
_____

| Monday | | Thursday | |
|---|---|---|---|
| Tuesday | | Friday | |
| Wednesday | | Saturday | |
| | | Sunday | |

# Weekly Planner

| | | | |
|---|---|---|---|
| Monday | | Friday | |
| Tuesday | | Saturday | |
| Wednesday | | Sunday | |
| Thursday | | | |

things to do

_____

_____

_____

_____

_____

_____

things to buy

_____

_____

_____

_____

_____

_____

Notes

_____

_____

_____

_____

_____

_____

# Weekly Planner

things to do

_____
_____
_____
_____
_____
_____

things to buy

_____
_____
_____
_____
_____

Notes

_____
_____
_____
_____
_____
_____

Monday

Tuesday

Wednesday

Thursday

Friday

Saturday

Sunday

# 03 *March*

Weekly Planner

Monday

Friday

Tuesday

Saturday

Wednesday

Sunday

Thursday

things to do

_____
_____
_____
_____
_____
_____
_____

things to buy

_____
_____
_____
_____
_____
_____
_____

Notes

_____
_____
_____
_____
_____

# Weekly Planner

things to do

_____

_____

_____

_____

_____

_____

_____

things to buy

_____

_____

_____

_____

_____

Notes

_____

_____

_____

_____

_____

_____

| Monday | | Thursday | |
| Tuesday | | Friday | |
| Wednesday | | Saturday | |
| | | Sunday | |

# Weekly Planner

| Monday | | Friday |
|--------|--|--------|
| Tuesday | | Saturday |
| Wednesday | | Sunday |
| Thursday | | |

things to do

_____

_____

_____

_____

_____

_____

_____

things to buy

_____

_____

_____

_____

_____

_____

_____

Notes

_____

_____

_____

_____

_____

_____

# Weekly Planner

things to do

_____
_____
_____
_____
_____
_____
_____

things to buy

_____
_____
_____
_____
_____

Notes

_____
_____
_____
_____
_____
_____

Monday

Tuesday

Wednesday

Thursday

Friday

Saturday

Sunday

# 04 April

| | |
|---|---|
| **Monday** | **Friday** |
| **Tuesday** | **Saturday** |
| **Wednesday** | **Sunday** |
| **Thursday** | |

**things to do**

_____
_____
_____
_____
_____
_____
_____

**things to buy**

_____
_____
_____
_____
_____
_____

**Notes**

_____
_____
_____
_____
_____
_____

# Weekly Planner

things to do

_____
_____
_____
_____
_____
_____
_____

things to buy

_____
_____
_____
_____
_____
_____

Notes

_____
_____
_____
_____
_____
_____

Monday

Tuesday

Wednesday

Thursday

Friday

Saturday

Sunday

# Weekly Planner

| Monday | | Friday | |
|---|---|---|---|
| Tuesday | | Saturday | |
| Wednesday | | Sunday | |
| Thursday | | | |

things to do

_____
_____
_____
_____
_____
_____
_____

things to buy

_____
_____
_____
_____
_____
_____

Notes

_____
_____
_____
_____
_____
_____

# Weekly Planner

things to do

_____

_____

_____

_____

_____

_____

things to buy

_____

_____

_____

_____

_____

Notes

_____

_____

_____

_____

_____

_____

Monday

Tuesday

Wednesday

Thursday

Friday

Saturday

Sunday

| Monday | | Friday | |
|---|---|---|---|
| **Tuesday** | | **Saturday** | |
| **Wednesday** | | **Sunday** | |
| **Thursday** | | | |

things to do

_____
_____
_____
_____
_____
_____
_____

things to buy

_____
_____
_____
_____
_____
_____

Notes

_____
_____
_____
_____
_____
_____

# Weekly Planner

things to do

_____

_____

_____

_____

_____

_____

things to buy

_____

_____

_____

_____

Notes

_____

_____

_____

_____

_____

_____

Monday

Tuesday

Wednesday

Thursday

Friday

Saturday

Sunday

# Weekly Planner

| | | |
|---|---|---|
| **Monday** | | **Friday** |
| **Tuesday** | | **Saturday** |
| **Wednesday** | | **Sunday** |
| **Thursday** | | |

## things to do

_____

_____

_____

_____

_____

_____

_____

## things to buy

_____

_____

_____

_____

_____

_____

_____

## Notes

_____

_____

_____

_____

_____

_____

# Weekly Planner

things to do

_____
_____
_____
_____
_____
_____

things to buy

_____
_____
_____
_____
_____

Notes

_____
_____
_____
_____
_____
_____

Monday

Tuesday

Wednesday

Thursday

Friday

Saturday

Sunday

# 06 June

| Monday | | Friday | |
|---|---|---|---|
| Tuesday | | Saturday | |
| Wednesday | | Sunday | |
| Thursday | | | |

things to do

_____
_____
_____
_____
_____
_____
_____

things to buy

_____
_____
_____
_____
_____
_____

Notes

_____
_____
_____
_____
_____

# Weekly Planner

things to do

_____
_____
_____
_____
_____
_____
_____

things to buy

_____
_____
_____
_____
_____
_____
_____

Notes

_____
_____
_____
_____
_____
_____
_____

Monday

Tuesday

Wednesday

Thursday

Friday

Saturday

Sunday

# Weekly Planner

Monday

Tuesday

Wednesday

Thursday

Friday

Saturday

Sunday

things to do

things to buy

Notes

# Weekly Planner

things to do

_____
_____
_____
_____
_____
_____
_____

things to buy

_____
_____
_____
_____
_____
_____

Notes

_____
_____
_____
_____
_____
_____
_____

Monday

Tuesday

Wednesday

Thursday

Friday

Saturday

Sunday

# Weekly Planner

## Grocery List

_____
_____
_____
_____
_____

## Reminders

_____
_____
_____
_____
_____
_____
_____
_____
_____
_____
_____
_____

## Contact Number

_____
_____
_____
_____
_____

## Notes

# Weekly Planner

## Grocery List

_____
_____
_____
_____
_____

## Contact Number

_____
_____
_____
_____
_____
_____

## Reminders

_____ _____ _____
_____ _____ _____
_____ _____ _____
_____ _____ _____
_____ _____ _____
_____ _____ _____
_____ _____ _____
_____ _____ _____
_____ _____ _____
_____ _____ _____
_____ _____ _____
_____ _____ _____

## Notes

www.ingramcontent.com/pod-product-compliance
Lightning Source LLC
Chambersburg PA
CBHW081335090426
42737CB00017B/3147